To Mike

Love
Sherena

Baseball from the Ground Up

Baseball from the Ground Up

John Oliveria
with
Douglas J. DeLisa

VANTAGE PRESS
New York

FIRST EDITION

All rights reserved, including the right of
reproduction in whole or in part in any form.

Copyright © 1993 by John Oliveria and Douglas J. DeLisa

Published by Vantage Press, Inc.
516 West 34th Street, New York, New York 10001

Manufactured in the United States of America
ISBN: 0-533-10411-4

Library of Congress Catalog Card No.: 92-93864

0 9 8 7 6 5 4 3 2 1

To God, who has blessed me so much in my life; for my wife, may the good Lord have a place on his team for her; and my daughter, Vicky, thank you for your love and support over the years; and to Brooks Robinson, who showed me the levels of strength and determination an individual can achieve

Johnny O.

Without John Oliveria, a fountain of baseball knowledge, I still would be dreaming about my first book. John's journey through baseball time, his friends, insights, and compassion for the game, have made this book a very enjoyable project for me.

I would like to recognize all who helped shape the writer I am; primarily my parents, Joseph and Jean, and the teacher who helped a class clown mature, Jeannie Wilson. I would like to especially thank my wife, Stacy, for being by my side and keeping the faith; our beautiful new daughter, Chanelle Rose; and God for providing me with the strength and spirit, who has made everything possible in my life.

Douglas J. DeLisa

Contents

Foreword by Brooks Robinson   ix

One. The St. Louis Browns   1
Two. Scouting, Texas League   6
Three. Cocoa Astros, Richmond Braves   11
Four. Texas Rangers   37
Five. Being a Groundskeeper   48
Six. My Favorite Players   55

References   69

Foreword

Baseball from the Ground Up lets us take an inside view of our national pastime from within the baseball scenes. John shows us just how fast things can change within the structure of an organization. John examines all the little subtleties of the game and insights on field conditions that can help win a game for you. John is a man who has experienced every phase of the game, from head groundkeeper to general manager.

I have many of the same memories that John has, and reading his book brought back a lot of nice memories for me—I think the world of John.

Brooks Robinson

One
The St. Louis Browns

I was eighteen years old back in New Bedford, Massachusetts, in 1936, and you could hardly find a job in those days. I liked being around people and started marathon dancing for the George L. Rudy Company. This only lasted about three months before I picked up in the big band circuit under the name of Reggie Stevens. We played warmups on Sunday nights for big performers like Fletcher Henderson, Count Basie, Jimmy Lundsford, and Ina Ray Hutton.

Growing up in Massachusetts, I was a big Red Sox fan, and my favorite players were Dominic DiMaggio and Bobby Doerr. I moved to Mason City, Iowa, and started selling fertilizer and sod door-to-door. One day while selling sod from the side of the road, I met Bob Feller's mom and even Joe Hatton. He lived in Bankroft, Iowa, home to one of the teams I was about to play for. Baseball was my greatest love! I played in a semiprofessional league for Algona, Iowa, when I was twenty-two years old. I was a pitcher and better-than-average hitter. We played teams from Blue Earth and Austin, Minnesota, and it was a pretty good league.

After a couple of years of semipro ball, I spotted an ad in the *Des Moines Register* that would change my life forever. The ad read: "Wanted, Baseball Scout," for the St. Louis Browns. Hugh Lott, who was the head scout, was looking for a part-time scout or, as it was called in those days, a "bird dog." Well, I went to St. Louis for an interview and to my surprise was hired on the spot. Well, anyway, bird dogs in those days weren't paid wages but instead got paid signing bonuses. A players were so much, Double A players more, and Triple A players even more.

The St. Louis Browns weren't drawing any crowds because the Cardinals were the main attraction in St. Louis. Brown's owner Bill Veck was trying to move the club to Baltimore, Maryland, unsuccessfully, because the American League owners wouldn't allow the club to move. Bill Veck was not a exceptionally wealthy man, so he ended up selling the better players to keep the Browns alive. He even sold most of his established players just to pay the bills.

I was really enthusiastic about my job and ran several tryout camps throughout the Midwest. I covered Iowa, Wisonsin, Illinois, and Minnesota. When Hugh Lott was stepping down, he recommended me for his position as head scout with St. Louis. I got the job, which paid $300 per month plus expenses; that was good money in those days.

In 1943, Bill Veck was forced to sell the club to a group of businessmen in Baltimore. Art Eilers was appointed general manager in Baltimore, and they kept me on for another year. The group owning the club then wanted to hire a big-name general manager, and the next year Paul Richards took over. They also made him the field manager. At that time Paul had a friend, a former pitcher from the major leagues, Phil Gallivan, and of course he wanted Phil to take over scouting duties in my area. Now baseball is just like politics, where you bring your friends in. So one day Paul told me, "Johnny, you have experience in landscaping. How about you going down to San Antonio and taking over the grounds there? The grounds are in real bad shape, and that's a Double A ball club there."

Well, I was really disappointed and it took me some time to think things over. I realized that if I wanted to keep my foot in baseball, I'd better take up residence in San Antonio. So I did, and to my surprise it was the best thing to ever happen to me in baseball.

Scouting, it's a very lonely job with the daily traveling as well as endless and nameless motels. I had bought a brand-new car and put 50,000 miles on it by the end of the year.

Well, in the fall of 1954 I went to San Antonio and worked for the Baltimore Orioles' Double A club. I had never been a groundskeeper before, and my first look at my new job was a very disappointing one, indeed, I walked into Mission Stadium and I wanted to turn around and go back home. No trimmed grass, brown spots everywhere, and a rock quarry for an infield, what a mess! But by spring it was a different story; Mission Stadium was now a beautiful field in excellent playing condition. I accomplished this by completely resodding the infield along with replacing all the dirt on the infield, to start with, and reworking the sidelines.

At that time, I had five people working for me, but the one person that stood out was a fella named Felix Trevino. Felix really knew his job, and he actually taught me the art of groundskeeping. He did a really great job for me. Thanks, Felix.

I was really happy in San Antonio, because taking care of the grounds had me home every night. In fact, I ate all my lunches at home and played golf every day. The minor leagues in those days were not drawing too many people, whereas today minor league clubs are flourishing and being bought and sold for millions of dollars. In those days you couldn't get anything for them and actually you were doing somebody a favor if you took over the club.

During those days, in the Texas League we had some pretty good ball players come and go, Brooks Robinson, Ron Hansen, and Ryne Duren, to name a few. We had a manager at that time named Don Heffner, and Paul Richards didn't like Don too well. At that time the club was called the San Antonio Missions, and at the end of the year Don and the club finished a half-game out of first place. Of course Paul didn't think that was good enough. About that time, Paul sent his scout to San Antonio to check on his players, and Don didn't like that too much. Paul then sent Lou Fitzgerald down to San Antonio to manage the following season.

I stayed on in San Antonio for a few more years, and then Baltimore decided to sell the ball club and park. In the meantime, the Chicago Cubs wanted to lease the ballpark and join the Texas League, so they put a Double A club in San Antonio. While all of this was happening, Baltimore was still trying to make up their minds whether or not to sell the park. Meanwhile, the Cubs leased the park that year and had some really good players working there like Billy Williams, Ron Santo, and Ron Perranoski. Mr. Wrigley, owner of the Chicago club, had the revoluntionary idea of revolving managers, and San Antonio was its testing grounds. He sent managers down for one or two months at a time, the likes of which included Chuck Kline and Bobby Adams, but Mr. Wrigley was never quite satisfied.

That year you could also sign ball players that were, so to speak, in the twilight of their careers, so we signed Howie Fox. Well, at the end of the season Howie retired and opened a beer garden in South San Antonio. One night, these two hoodlums came in right at closing time. Howie explained it was closing time, but the two kids came in and sat with his wife and daughter anyway. Howie said, "You have to leave; we're closing," and the kids left. The next thing you know, rocks were hitting the front door and Howie went out to see what was going on. All of a sudden, Howie fell into the doorway of his beer garden, stabbed in the stomach and bleeding to death in front of his wife and daughter. The next day Ryne Duren and I cleaned up the blood. The hoodlums were eventually caught but only received five years in prison for stabbing Howie Fox to death.

The Cubs stayed in San Antonio for another two years and then finally decided to pull out. A fellow by the name of Danny Sullivan took over the ball club. I called a friend of mine, Dick King, on Danny's behalf and asked if he would be interested in a general manager's job in San Antonio. At the time of the call, Dick was in Mexico, scouting for the Cincinnati Reds, and said he was interested in the job. Dick came to San Antonio, and that fall Dick King and I went to St. Petersburg, Florida, for the winter baseball convention. It was at this time that Danny Sullivan named Dick King as the general manager of the San Antonio club.

Two
Scouting, Texas League

Scouting was not one of my favorite jobs, but I signed with Charlie Hurth to scout for the New York Mets in 1960. Now scouting in Texas was like driving across the United States. I would call to New York and they would say, "Johnny, go out to Paris, Texas, and look at this Floyd Weaver, a pitcher with a big arm." When I arrived in Paris I would call the main office and they would tell me to go to El Paso to look at some kid that was playing there the following night.

Charlie Hurth left the club halfway through the season and George Weiss, who was the executive manager with the New York Yankees, was hired by the Mets and I stayed on scouting for the Mets. Now George didn't know me, so he sent Red Ruffing, a former Yankees pitcher, to ride around with me for a couple of weeks to see if I knew anything about major league talent.

I took Red to Paris, Texas, and showed him Floyd Weaver. I took Red to Houston, were I showed him a kid by the name of Steve Cosgrove; then we went to San Antonio and I showed him two players I liked, Jerry Grote, and Davey Johnson. We went to the ball game that night. Trinity University was playing San Antonio, and Dell Baker, a coach from the Boston Red Sox, was helping the coach at Trinity. He took us out to dinner that night after the game and asked Red Ruffing, "Red, why don't you let John sign Jerry Grote and Davey Johnson?"

Now after we left Dell Baker's house, Red and I got into the car and Red said, "John, don't pay any attention to Dell Baker; he can't see too good anymore." Then Red laughed. A week later he went back to New York and told George Weiss he didn't think I knew too much about talent. So I was let go at the end of the season.

In the fall of 1961, after being let go by the New York Mets, I returned to San Antonio. Dick King was still there as general manager for the Chicago Cubs Double A club in San Antonio, and he called and hired me as the head groundskeeper for the next season. This would be the the Cubs' last year in San Antonio. They had a pretty fair team featuring Billy Williams, Ron Perranoski, and Ron Santo.

In 1962 the Houston Astros bought Mission Stadium in San Antonio and put their Double A ball club in there. Now Spec Richardson was the general manager for Houston at the time. Spec sent Grady Hatton in to manage the team in San Antonio.

When the Astros were in San Antonio, Texas, we had some great talent there. There were Joe Morgan, Rusty Staub, Jimmy Wynn, Sonny Jackson, Larry Dirker, and Don Wilson, all very talented ball players. We also had Doug Rader on third base; he was outstanding. They moved Doug up to the Astros and I kept meeting Doug at all the spring training programs and we became close friends. There was a lot of talent here, and the Astros won the Texas League title two years in a row. Then the Astros hired a general manager named Ward Goodrich and Ward talked Spec Richardson into moving the club to Amarillo, Texas. When Spec moved the ball club to Amarillo he asked me, "John, how would you like to go to Florida and take over the brand-new spring training facility being built in Cocoa, Florida?" Well, right there I decided to stay in baseball, so I moved to Cocoa, Florida.

In 1963, when I came to Cocoa, the fields had just been

built. We had four ballparks and one stadium where the major league ball players trained. The four minor league fields were for AAA, AA, and two Single A clubs to train. I was in charge of the fields there; I reconditioned, fertilized, and seeded those fields. And they became some pretty good ballparks. We had a 5,000-seat stadium and a 101-room dormitory. The dormitory housed all the major league players, and I stayed there with the Astros.

I remember one night Dave Philley, who used to play for the Philadelphia Phillies, suspected that some of the ball players were coming back to the dorms well after curfew. They were climbing up the pole that led to the TV antenna to the top of the building and sneaking in through the skylight window. Dave decided to play a little trick on them, and he greased the pole about halfway up. So now these ball players coming in late would climb up that pole and get to the greasy spot and would slide back down again. Then they would have to come in the front door and we knew everyone who was breaking curfew.

Don Zimmer told me a story one year when he was the manager for the Key West club. It seemed that his bus driver liked to do a little drinking and on their way back down to Key West he was driving on and off the road. It must have gotten pretty bad, because Don finally told him to "Stop this damn bus!" Then he hollered to the players, "Does anyone know how to drive this thing?" Well, one of the ball players came up and took over and they made it back to Key West, but that was the end of the line for the bus driver; Don had him terminated. Don didn't really like that job very much, because it was a long way down through the Keys and a lot of traveling in the Florida State League.

In 1967, Art Perkins was the general manager in Cocoa and was promoted to the traveling secretary position in Houston. In 1968 Spec Richardson asked me to take over the general manager's job in Cocoa. Now Art never did much promoting and only drew about 300- 400 people per game, somewhere around 5,553 people total. Now numbers like that don't pay the bills, so I brought in a grand promotional campaign. I brought the local business community in so the city of Cocoa could feel more involved with the Astros. We gave away everything from free tickets to a complete stereo system.

I remember one night while the game was in progress, Cesar Cedeno came running into the dugout and didn't want to go back out into the field. Everyone was wondering what was going on. Then Ray Busse, our right fielder, took a bat out to the outfield and killed a five-foot rattlesnake and brought it into the dugout. Pat Gillick took the snake, and the next day he went to Melbourne, Florida, had it skinned, and had a belt made out of it. Pat Gillick is now the general manager for the Toronto Blue Jays.

Old Judge Hoffeinz owned an old bus that he built for the minor league club. I used to keep it parked near the dormitory, and of all people, I was the lucky one who had to drive the bus. I never drove a bus in my life, and I remember taking a busload of players to play at Miami one night. I was scared to death. We played the Fort Lauderdale Yankees and came back home after a three-day stay. Then we had a trip to Lakeland and we played a good ball game that night. On our way back there was nothing but woods, marshes, and swamps between St. Cloud and Cocoa on Highway 532. I'll be darned if the bus didn't break down halfway between St. Cloud and Cocoa. Here we were, two o'clock in the morning, in complete darkness in the middle of swampland with no place to go. Some of the players got tired of waiting on the bus and started to walk. I wouldn't walk because I was afraid of snakes crossing the highway at night. You never know, because Highway 532 is surrounded by swamps. Who knows what's crawling around at night? So I slept on the bus that night. Walt Matthews and a couple of other ball players stayed on the bus. About fifteen of the ball players hitchhiked all the way back to Cocoa. A car would come down Highway 532 maybe once every thirty minutes or so, and most of the players managed to get rides.

The next morning I had to call Cocoa and imform them that the bus was broken down between St. Cloud and Cocoa. The garage came and towed us in and kept us there all day long before they finally got the bus fixed. Now, the snakes would come and lie out on the asphalt where the road was nice and warm from the sun all day long. I stayed on the bus until it was fixed and time to leave.

We had an outstanding team in Cocoa. I had Walt Matthews and Tony Pechecco as managers along with outstanding playing talent. There were John Mayberry, Bob Watson, Cesar Cedeno, Cesar Geronimo, and James Rodney Richards, who later became a great pitcher with the Houston Astros but had to retire early because of a minor stroke he had in Houston, as the doctors wouldn't allow him to play baseball any longer. My batboy at the time was Clint Hurdle.

Yes, in 1968 when I was hired as general manager I was determined to make the team flourish in Cocoa. My attendance goal was 15,000, and with all the promotions I worked on, I knew I would make it. That year the final attendance figures reached 28,923, a gain of 421 percent over the '67 season. This was the greatest percentage of increase ever recorded in the Minor Leagues National Association. I was given the honor of being chosen the Executive of the Year in the Florida State League and receiving the Larry McPhail Award for the best promotions and the Grand Sweepstakes Award for the greatest percentage of increase in attendance.

Three
Cocoa Astros, Richmond Braves

Spec Richardson was a great person to work for. He cared about people, and he was a team player. Spec even built a recreation building with pool tables. We had a sixty-foot piece of Astroturf from Monsanto Chemicals where the players went through their morning exercises. Spec had a big pond built in back of the recreation building, and the Fish and Game Commission stocked the pond with lots of fish so the players could relax and fish after their workouts.

The people were really supporting exhibition games pretty well in Cocoa, especially when the Yankees, Dodgers, and Cardinals came into town. But in 1971 I was dealt a bad deal from Tal Smith, who came to work for the Astros that year. I had a run-in with Tal when he was our farm director at one time, and I made it quite clear that I was not a Tal Smith fan. The Miami Marlins were in town, and their manager, Woody Smith, had his son up for the game. Now Woody's son was kicking a soccer ball up against the batting cage. I hollered over at him to stop, but he couldn't hear me 'cause I was about six hundred feet away. I grabbed a .410 shotgun and fired it in the air to get his attention. Consequently he heard it and ran in and told his dad that I took a shot at him. Now even if I had taken a shot at him, there is no way a .410 shotgun could fire six hundred feet.

Now Tal Smith's snoop was in town that night, and he took

the report and called down to Houston and talked to Tal Smith about this incident. Tal Smith didn't want to give the report to Spec Richardson because Spec would just have a little talk with me. Tal Smith filed papers with the lawyers at the Astrodome. They put the report on our attorney's desk and they had me. Spec came to Cocoa, and two days later they had me in a hospital in Texas, where I stayed for three days while they were examining me. Finally, the team doctor told Spec, "There's nothing wrong with John; just send him back to Cocoa." But the attorney, along with Tal Smith, said they couldn't send me back to Cocoa, that they would have to let me go. So I was fired from the Astros organization, but I was actually ready to go, because I had been offered a job with the new Global League at twice the salary I was making in Cocoa by Mr. Dilbeck.

Happy Chandler was going to be the commissioner for the upstart Global League. He had me riding around San Francisco in his big limousine with his chauffeur, trying to impress me to get me to go to the Global League. But limousines didn't really impress me; I had my feet on the ground. At the time Mr. Dilbeck owned the Louisville franchise in the National Association and he also owned Rock Hill in the Western Carolina League and was probably the only person that wanted to own an entire league.

The Global League was scheduled to hold spring training in Daytona Beach prior to starting its 140-game schedule. There were going to be six teams, including Jersey City, which was going to be my team, and franchises in New Orleans, Louisiana; Caracas, Venezuela; Puerto Rico; and two clubs in Japan. This was supposed to be a really swinging league, with some of the games being played in large non–major league cities like Miami and Dallas. In order to make a success of this new venture, Mr. Dilbeck was trying to surround himself with some of the more well known people in baseball. He signed Roy Campanella as manager and Johnny Mize as batting coach for Jersey City. Campy's pitching coach would be none other than his old battery mate Don Newcombe. Dilbeck not only wanted to run the best teams on the field, but he wanted the best executives. He was after me and in fact offered me a three-year contract worth $20,000 a year, a lot more than ol' Judge Hoffeinz was paying me in that million-dollar complex in Cocoa. You would think that I would have jumped at the chance, but I didn't. I said, "The Global League hasn't gotten off the ground, and I've got more friends than you can count," so I passed up the Global League and was offered a job in Elmira, New York, working for Joe Romano. I worked for Joe about three months before I quit. This guy was one of the most cost-conscious guys I ever ran into. Joe had kids sweeping the ball park and at the end of the day he would give them each a free ticket to the game and twenty-five cents. On Opening Day he had a line of five hundred people with one ticket office open and only one ticket salesperson. I mean this guy was really thrifty. I didn't appreciate that, so I quit and left for home.

On my way home I stopped in Richmond and visited with the general manager of the Triple A Atlanta Braves club, Roger Borttorff. Roger asked me if I would be interested in taking over the ballpark in Richmond because it was in really bad shape. I told Roger that I would let him know.

By the time I returned home to Cocoa, Florida, Joe Ryan of the Miami Marlins asked me if I would be interested in the general manager position with Miami. Now Miami had a working agreement with the Baltimore Orioles, so I told Joe that I'd give it a try. I went to Miami and tried selling some advertising on the fence signs and the box seats. In the meantime Roger Borttorff called my home in Cocoa and my wife told him that I wasn't there, but she'd have me call him back. In this day and age most of the people in Miami spoke Spanish, and I didn't speak the language. So I wasn't very successful. After a couple of months I figured I'd just go home.

As soon as I returned to Cocoa I called Roger and he offered me the head groundskeeper/field superintendent position in Richmond. I took the job as head groundskeeper, and believe me, that park was a shambles. The outfield was filled with bad grass and dandelions, the infield was a rockpile, so I decided to resod the outfield and put in new dirt in the infield. The ball park at this time was named Parker Field, and it became one of the better ball parks in the International League.

That year we had Joe Niekro, whose brother Phil Niekro was pitching for the Atlanta Braves at the time. Joe ended up being called up to Atlanta that year; they had some good years there. We had a couple of good players in Richmond, Frank LaCorte, a pitcher that later went to the Braves, and a young kid named Dale Murphy.

Then in 1973 Roger quit as general manager and took a job running the Tobacco Festival in Richmond. It was like the Rose Bowl Parade, with big floats, and was sponsored by the tobacco companies during the fall. So the Atlanta Braves asked me if I would be interested in being the general manager. Needless to say, I took the job. I had Clint "Scraps" Courtney as my manager, and my pitching coach was Johnny Sain. Now remember, Johnny Sain pitched for the Boston Braves with Warren Spahn. Both Johnny and Warren were twenty-game winners, and the saying in Boston was, "Spahn and Sain and pray for rain."

In the middle of the year Clint Courtney was in Rochester, New York, when he had a heart attack and passed away while playing Ping-Pong with the players in the hotel lobby. The Braves immediately sent Bob Lemon, former Cleveland Indians pitcher, to finish the year managing in Richmond.

A local radio man visited me one day at Parker Field. He said on his radio show something like this: "Parker Field looks strange in late October. The grass is not quite as green, the net protecting spectators from foul balls is down. Another one is expected to be put up, one which the ball won't sail through into the stands. It's chilly out here, and the wind is blowing. You see, supposedly John Oliveria was hit in his soft spot about six weeks ago, when a new edition came to Parker Field. As a matter of fact, five new editions! A most attractive black and white stray dog decided to give John some company during the off season. It was less than five minutes into my October tour around the stands that John started looking under steps and behind barrels. I thought the loneliness had affected John just a bit, and then he muttered something about, 'She moved them again.' At first I thought John's secretary must have hidden something which John stashed somewhere; then I discovered he meant the five puppies and the stray, who we'll now refer to as 'Momma.' Thank goodness we found them about fifteen minutes later, or we'd probably still be looking for them. So old John's been saving food for Momma, making places for her and her puppies to sleep. Old tough John Oliveria has been keeping Momma fed so she can feed the offspring. John says he doesn't want to send them to the pound, that he'd rather give them away to someone. I guess it's only proper to let you people of Richmond know that it's a cute little puppy and especially if you're a Parker Field fan, old John has five to give away. Don't tell him I told you, but you can reach John at 359-4444." Needless to say, I got rid of the puppies really quick. People were calling in from all over Richmond wanting one of those puppies.

 The following year I had Jack McKeon as my manager and again Johnny Sain was my pitching coach. We had some very interesting promotions. Why, one night we gave away nine cars, one every inning. Needless to say, we had a pretty good night. We drew 7,000 people, and that was a pretty good night in those days. Today 7,000 is not a very big crowd in some of those Triple A cities.

 Ted Turner arrived in Richmond. I met him at the airport,

and he gave me that "How ya doing, man," and one of those big high fives. He got in the car and I drove him over to the ball park. I told him to take my car and go to the motel, and pointed him in the right direction. I told him that he had reservations at the Holiday Inn. I said, "You go ahead and take my car; just bring it back when you come to the game tonight and you can use it while you're here."

Ted said, "That's fine, Johnny." He took the car and drove off. That night he came to the ball game and one of our players hit a home run and Ted ran out on the field and gave him a big hug. Now, Ted really gets excited during the ball games.

Anyway, at the end of that year my contract was not renewed at Richmond. John Richardson, who was an aggressive promotion director in Atlanta, wanted the job in Richmond. He did a good job in Atlanta, so they sent him to Richmond and I lost my job because of that.

George Bush, Jr.

Yogi Berra and John

Rusty Staub

John Oliveria when he had a band under the name Reggie Stevens

Schoolboy Rowe and John

Spec Richardson and Harry "The Hat" Walker

Brooks Robinson

Sparky Lyle

Bobby Valentine

Toby Harrah

Gaylord Perry

Mickey Mantle

Bob Feller and John

Sal Maglie

Billy Hunter

Wayne Terwilliger

Jim Wynn

Rick Honeycutt

Johnny Pesky and John

Rogers Hornsby and John

Gene Mauch and John

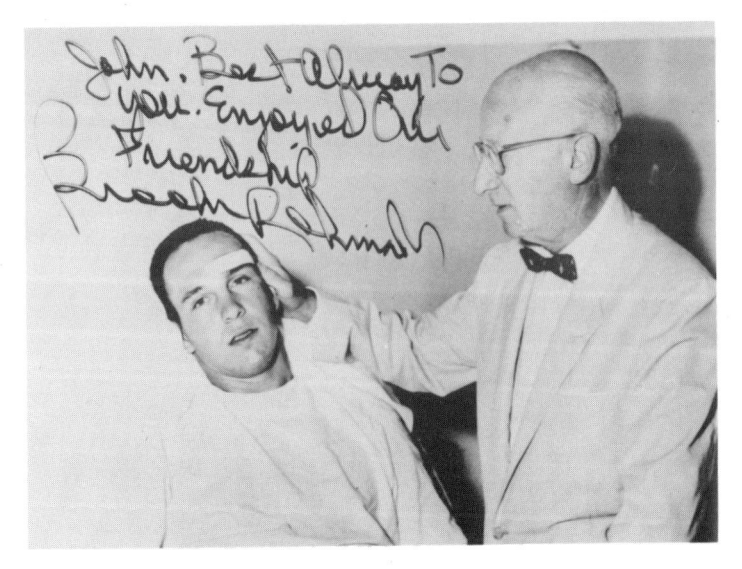

Brooks Robinson
Photograph courtesy of the Baltimore Orioles

San Antonio Missions team picture 1955. *Bottom row, far left, Star McIlvaine, general manager; top row, fourth from left, Ryan Duran; top row, sixth from left, Howie Fox; top row, eleventh from left, Frank Fanovich.*

Joe Macko

Joe Morgan

Tommy Helms, John, and Don Zimmer

John Oliveria

Bucky Dent and John

Buddy Bell and John

Brooks Robinson in San Antonio

Jim Sunberg and John

Four
Texas Rangers

I returned home to Cocoa, Florida, and my wife told me that Eddie Robinson and Danny O'Brian were calling me from Arlington, Texas. They wanted me to go down to Arlington, so my wife and I decided it would be a good idea to take a ride and see what this was all about. I'd never been a major league groundskeeper before, although I did turn down three jobs in the major leagues. So we hauled off to Arlington, Texas.

At Arlington, Eddie Robinson was the general manager. I worked for Eddie when he was with the Atlanta Braves. Eddie was the person who sent me to Richmond. So I was very excited to be working for someone who had feelings toward their help, as Eddie always treated his help well. Brad Corbett was the owner of the Rangers. He was having a tough time making ends meet, so we were on a tight budget as far as expenditures were concerned. Before I took the job as head groundskeeper for the Rangers, they went through three groundskeepers in the previous three years. I immediately resodded the whole outfield with 419 Bermuda grass, changed the dirt in the infield, and put in a brand-new sprinkler system. The sprinkler system that is there now is the same one I put in in 1976.

Our manager at the time was Frank Lucchesi. Frank was a good man to work with, but the following year Mr. Corbett let Frank go, hired Connie Ryan as interim manager for a couple of days, let him go, and hired Eddie Stanky and Eddie managed the Rangers for one day. Eddie was in front of the dugout and he passed out before the ball game, so he didn't even get a chance to manage. As a matter of fact, I helped carry him off the field on a stretcher. The next day Eddie decided he didn't even want the job and quit. Mr. Corbett then hired Billy Hunter, and he stayed with the Rangers a couple of years. Billy Hunter was the one who got me in trouble with Billy Martin. You see, whenever Billy came into town he would check the field like a doctor checks his patients. He would roll a ball down the base paths to see if the ball would roll fair or foul, then inspect the pitcher's mound. Now, Billy Hunter always had me fooling around with home plate.

One night when Billy Martin and the Yankees were in town, Rick Honeycutt was pitching for the Rangers and Billy Hunter told me, "John, Honeycutt's pitching tonight, so soften up that home plate a little bit." So I put a ton of sand around home plate, because Rick Honeycutt is a sinkerball pitcher and with sinkerballers when the batter swings at the ball he has a tendency to top the ball. Now if the area around home plate is hard, the ball with bounce over the pitcher's head into center field for a base hit. So as Billy was inspecting the field conditions before the game, he checked out home plate and he was getting really angry. So Billy went to the dugout and got a ball, came back to the home plate area, and threw the ball down in front of home plate and the ball didn't bounce a half-inch.

Now coincidentally, Lee McPhail, the league president, just happened to be in the crowd that night, and Billy called him down out of the stands. Billy said, "Look here, Lee; look at this. It's just like a damn beach." Billy threw the ball down there, and the ball just went "plop" right into the sand.

So now Lee McPhail turned to me and said, "John, you've got to get this fixed. If you don't have this fixed by tomorrow night's game, you are going to have to forfeit the game."

Yes, Martin was really articulate about the playing field.

He would *always* come out early to the ballpark to check the grass, the base paths, the pitcher's mound, and home plate. I would have to say in my opinion throughout all my years in baseball, that Billy Martin was probably one of the smartest managers in baseball. Billy was tough, thorough, emphatic toward his players, always giving 100 percent, and he wouldn't back down from anyone. One thing I always tried to make sure was that if any of my players wanted the field in a certain way that may be illegal, I always refused to do it, but I can't honestly say that I didn't. Our utmost goal was to win ball games, and as a pitcher if you felt more comfortable with a mound a little higher than it was supposed to be, who was I to tell you no? Gaylord Perry was always accused of throwing a spitter, but there's no way in the world any other player could even know if he was, in fact, throwing an illegal pitch. To this day no one ever did find out, to the best of my knowledge, and I myself never saw anything illegal about Gaylord's pitching.

Brad Corbett eventually sold the franchise to Eddie Childes, who was a big baseball fan. He meant well and wanted the Rangers to win, but he didn't really have the baseball knowledge to run the franchise. In my opinion he made a lot of mistakes. He fired a lot of managers, I'd say about one a year. Well anyway, Eddie decided he wanted a new manager, so he asked Eddie Robinson to get a new manager. Eddie Robinson let Billy Hunter go and brought in Pat Corrales from coach to the manager position. Pat stayed on for another year, and our club didn't finish any better that next year. Once again, Eddie Childes fired Pat Corrales or, rather, had Eddie Robinson fire Pat and then they hired Don Zimmer. Don Zimmer is one of the outstanding managers in baseball, but halfway through the season Eddie Childes was ready for another change. Mr. Childes decided he had enough of Eddie Robinson and scheduled a press conference on the track in front of the home dugout and told the press he was going to fire Eddie Robinson. Mr. Childes said, "Eddie Robinson has done a good job, but it is time to make some changes." Well, that immediately left an opening for the press and they asked, "If Eddie is doing such a good job, why are you letting him go?" Mr. Childes was at a loss for words.

The season continued and we were going along really well with Don Zimmer, but just before the end of the season Mr. Childes again decided he wanted to make a change in managers. Mr. Childes fired Don Zimmer and then changed his mind and asked Don if he would stay on for a couple of days until they could find a replacement. Then a couple of days later Darrel Johnson took over as manager for Don Zimmer. Darrel had been a third base coach with the Rangers, and he finished out the season with us.

The next season Mr. Childes brought in Mike Stone from the Western Company as executive vice president for the Rangers. It was Mr. Stone's desire to turn the Rangers' fortunes around. Apparently bleary-eyed from watching teams that had a finishing average of nineteen and a half games out of first place in each of the last five seasons, Mike Stone was trying to rid the franchise of this kind of image. The Rangers decided to build for the future from the ground up, and I was the chief architect, with my rake in hand. Mr. Stone made Joe Kline the general manager and Tom Grieve the farm director. Mr. Childes and Mr. Stone finally named Doug Rader the team manager. There was a lot of second-guessing going on in the front office. Joe Kline was second-guessing every deal that was made. Tom Grieve had aspirations of becoming the general manager, and as a matter of fact he is currently the general manager of the Texas Rangers. Mr. Childes hired Sam Mason as promotions director, and he was in charge of putting people in the ballpark and promoting the Rangers. A new infrastructure was built and put into place for the next season.

I had again been asked to perform my magic. This time I

was hoping they would send me to the new spring training complex in Port Charlotte. Mike Stone had invested a lot of money in the organization, especially in the younger players. That was where he felt the future lay with the club, and he wanted to do everything in his power to ensure their proper development. The Rangers would soon be breaking ground for a new minor league complex, and Mr. Stone asked me to go down and build the field. When Mike took over he didn't know much about baseball, but I thought he did a pretty good job. Mike was coming over to the ballpark every couple of days. I would stop by his office and say, "Mr. Stone, I hope Mr. Childes sees fit for you to go in here full-time. I enjoy working for you."

Things were going smoothly for us this year, and Sam Mason came out with a drink called Ranger-Aid. It was supposed to be like Gatorade. We had Ranger-Aid coming out of our ears; this stuff was all around the ballpark. Ball players had to have Ranger-Aid in the dugout; other soft drinks were no longer allowed. Ranger-Aid was the thing to drink. Sam tried to promote this throughout all the supermarkets in Arlington, but nobody would have any part of it. Consequently the Rangers dropped that piece of merchandise, but that lost the Rangers a lot of money. Sam tried to make a really big drink out of it, but instead it turned out to be a really big flop.

One big promotion that Sam Mason had was the Father-Son Ball Game. The fathers had to bat left-handed, and they all had their sons out there playing ball. This was a happy time. Some of the ball players had daughters, and they were out there, too. I remember Buddy Bell's little boy, because when it was time for them to get off the field, Buddy's little boy was still out there. So I shouted over to him, "C'mon, boys, let's get off the field!" The little Bell boy was still out there, so I went over to him and asked him if he would get off the field. I saw Buddy coming over to get him. I told Buddy that I didn't know this was his little boy. And then out of nowhere this cute little boy hauled off and punched me right in the nose. Now he was about five years old. Buddy didn't like that too much, but when we talked about it in the clubhouse he thought it was the funniest thing that ever happened to him. Actually, I thought it was pretty funny, how that little boy really hauled off and hit me.

I remember one evening when the Yankees were in town after the ball game Billy Martin decided to go out to a nightclub. Billy went out to the Lace Nite Club in Arlington. Billy went over there, had a few drinks, and got himself into some fisticuffs with some people at the club. Billy went to the bathroom, and some of the guys followed him in there and worked Billy over pretty good. It just happened that the Yankees were staying at the Hilton and that night the hotel had a fire and everyone was asked to evacuate the building. George Steinbrenner, the players, and all of the crew were outside, and now at 3:00 A.M, to their surprise, here comes Billy in a taxicab. Billy looked like he had been hit by a Texas tornado; he was all bruised up and looked like he was in really bad shape. Needless to say, George and the boys were really upset and I would have to say it was just a couple of weeks after that that George fired Billy again and replaced him with Lou Piniella.

Personally, I think Billy Martin was a real credit to baseball. He was a very colorful character; I enjoyed being around him. I enjoyed when he came into town because we always had to be on alert. There was never a dull moment with Billy Martin; I sure miss him.

One person I sure won't miss, and this is the only bad experience I've ever had in all my years in baseball. Some tractor company sent me an 8 X 10 picture of Reggie Jackson sitting on one of their tractors. They were trying to sell tractors, and I was in need of a couple sixteen-horsepower tractors, the ones that we used around the ballpark. One day in early July, when the California Angels were in town, Reggie Jackson was behind the batting cage waiting for his turn to hit before the game. So I took the picture to Reggie and asked if he would autograph it for me. Reggie jumped all over me. He told me to get lost, that he didn't want to autograph any pictures, and shouted for someone to get me out of there. So I tore up the picture in front of him and walked away from the batting cage. I thought, *If that's the way he feels, then I don't even want his picture.* Some of the sportswriters standing around asked me what happened. I told them I had a nice picture of Reggie and that I thought he might autograph it for me. I told them if Reggie wouldn't autograph it for me, then I didn't want it.

So now the next day the newspaper showed a big cartoon picture of Reggie with his arm outstretched telling me to get the hell away from him, with a big article on how he refused to autograph the picture for the field superintendent at Arlington Stadium.

The next day Reggie had just finished his batting practice and was in the outfield shagging fly balls. I was in my little golf cart by the dugout, and Reggie came running in asking me if I would like to have the picture autographed. He apologized several times, but I told him, "I'm sorry, Reggie, I destroyed that picture, but I'm glad you feel that way. I'm sorry I bothered you while you were getting ready for batting practice." Reggie said he was trying to concentrate on his pregame hitting and was tired of being bothered by autograph seekers. I accepted the apology, but in all my years in professional baseball, this was the only time any player came at me like that and for a few minutes I really didn't like the guy.

I realize now I shouldn't have bothered him when he was getting ready to take batting practice, but with my being on the field, I thought it would be all right for him to autograph that picture. If he was making money selling tractors, I didn't see how he could have been bothered by someone trying to get the picture autographed. I needed some tractors and I'm sure

I probably would have bought some from that company, but I immediately erased that thought because of Reggie's attitude.

I recently did my mailman a favor. It seems he was going to Toronto and wanted some tickets to the All-Star Game. He asked me if I knew anybody there who could get him some tickets. I said, "Well, I know Pat Gillick. I don't know if he can get you any tickets, because the commissioner of baseball has control of all the tickets." But I gave him Pat's name and number and told him to call Pat when he got to Toronto and maybe Pat could get him some tickets. Well, he went to Toronto and called Pat. Now I didn't know if Pat would remember me or not, but he sure did. Pat obliged my mailman by putting aside four free tickets at the press gate. My mailman happened to see Reggie Jackson there, because he was there on business. He asked Reggie if he could get his autograph, but Reggie said that he didn't want to be bothered. I know Reggie was a spectacular ball player, but I think signing autographs is part of the job. If no fans ever came to see Reggie or any other player, they wouldn't be worth a dime.

The next year Mike Stone brought in Larry Schmittou. Larry improved the ballpark a great deal by adding and improving the concessions. The only mistake I thought Larry made was when he put signs all around the ballpark saying that no food or drink was to be brought into the park. At several ball games the ticket takers were out there taking food away from the fans, the fans were complaining to the management, and when the management went to check, the ticket takers would already be eating the food. Well, Mr. Childes got a little perturbed about that, so he went all around the ballpark ripping all the signs down and that was the end of that. I liked working for Larry; he's a very successful businessman and a very successful baseball man.

Then Larry decided to bring in his own groundskeeper. He brought in Jim Anglia, who was a student at Vanderbilt when

Larry was coaching there. Jim had been a groundskeeper with Cleveland for one year, but he couldn't get along with the other groundskeeper there, so Larry brought him to Arlington. Larry got this bright idea to make me the field consultant. Larry said, "Johnny, I'd like to keep you so you can get your ten years in. Also, Mike Stone would like to see you get it so you can get a pretty good pension when you leave here." Now I wasn't really too happy about that, because I was really satisfied in Arlington. My wife lived here, we had a nice home, and things were just the way we liked them until this.

Now I had to do a lot of traveling. I went around to all the minor league ball parks and straightened them up. I had to travel to Burlington, Iowa, Oklahoma City, and Tulsa, Oklahoma. Oklahoma City's pitcher's mound was sixty feet long and it's supposed to be sixty feet, six inches. The mound is supposed to be ten inches high; this was fifteen inches high. You can see what a job I had on my hands, trying to fix minor league fields with minor league groundskeepers. I had to go to all those minor league clubs and show them how to fix the fields. I didn't like that too much because I had to do all of the work myself, as most of those groundskeepers were not familiar with building grounds. As a matter of fact, the three men they had fixing the grounds in Burlington, Iowa, were prisoners from the jail they would let out during the day to work on the field.

I checked the mounds at Burlington, and they were terrible. The pitching mound was sixty feet long, the visiting warm-up mound was sixty-five feet long, and the home warm-up mound was sixty feet long. This was a little out of the ordinary, because by the time a pitcher got readjusted to the distance he might have been in there for two or three innings.

But then Larry Schmittou asked me to go to Nashville to try and do something with that ballpark. I didn't think that was fair, because the Texas Rangers had nothing to do with the Nashville ball club. We had no working agreement with Nashville, and I felt I was being used. In the meantime the Texas Rangers were getting reimbursed by Larry for my services. After Nashville, I got a call from Larry asking me to go to Huntsville, Alabama, where he had just started a Double A ball club. When I arrived, to my surprise, there was no grass in the infield or outfield and there were two big holes dug at home plate and the pitcher's mound. The infield was terrible and there were about ten days until the start of the season. I worked really hard there, but the first couple of days it rained every day. Then finally on a Monday the weather became good. I started resodding the whole outfield and infield. I built the pitching mound, home plate, and the warning track. It kept me busy for the whole week, and by the time Friday rolled around it was Opening Day. (Incidentally, one of the ball players coming in there was Jose Canseco.) Larry was really pleased with the results at the ballpark there. Jose had a great year there and from there went on to Oakland.

Then I went back to Texas and Jim Anglia wanted me to water down the infield before the ball game. I didn't feel that was part of my job so I didn't do it. Brad Richards ended up watering down the infield; I guess Jim didn't want to do it or didn't know how to do it. Brad, being a former employee of mine, knew just how to do it. Actually, Brad does all the groundskeeping in Texas, because Jim has other outside activities. There's the Jim Anglia Turf Service, and he is the head groundskeeper for the Euliss Softball Complex. Also, Jim is busy building batting cages all over Arlington for organizations that want batting cages built.

Anyway, at the end of the year Larry Schmittou called me into his office and said that Mr. Stone wanted to talk to me. I went over to Mike Stone's office, and Mike said, "Johnny, the ball club had a pretty bad year and we're going to have to let you go." They continued my salary for another three months, and my salary ended March 1, which gave me exactly nine years and three months there.

It wasn't long after that when Mike Stone got fired for making some sly remarks about Mr. George Bush, Jr., who is now the owner of the Texas Rangers. Mike told Mr. Bush that all he wanted to do was take over the ball club and run it himself. Mr. Bush gave Mike six months' notice and then he would come in and take over. So Mike went to the newspapers and made some sly remarks. Mr. Bush came back to the ballpark and asked Mike to clean out his desk immediately. It did not hurt my feelings one bit, because I didn't think Mike had any reason to let me go just because the ball club had not drawn enough people. Anyway, the following year they signed Nolan Ryan, and since then the Rangers have been drawing about 2 million people a year.

The best thing to ever happen to the Texas Rangers was when George Bush, Jr., and his partners bought the ball club. Mr. Bush is a credit to baseball. He's liked by the fans and media, and he's doing a great job. Tom Grieve does a great job as general manager; he has a lot of experience in baseball. Tom has played with a lot of major league ball clubs. Tom's a great person to work for. He's kind and has a nice family, and I enjoyed working for him. I wish the Texas Rangers all the success in the world, because etched in my heart are a lot of great memories from the Texas Rangers family I'll love forever.

Five
Being a Groundskeeper

I would have to say that my biggest thrill being in baseball was not being a general manager or a scout, but being a head groundskeeper. When you are a good groundskeeper, your work shows. People come right up and tell you you're doing a good job, whereas if you're a general manager, of the hundreds or thousands of people in the stands nobody knows who you are. But if you have a really nice ballpark, the grass nice and green, the park well edged, you get recognition. And being the type of man that I am, I've always liked people and they've always told me, "Johnny O., you're doing a great job," and that's been really rewarding.

When I first went down to San Antonio for the Baltimore Orioles, the field was in really bad shape. I remember all the weeds in the outfield, the infield hard as a rock, but you can build all that up. I made a beautiful ballpark out of it. In San Antonio we could never afford good grass, so I would do the alternative. I always used a lot of fertilizer; consequently, my grass was always green, and San Antonio is a tough place to grow grass. I took the infield dirt, ran in some sand and some regular dirt, mixed them all together with my Rototiller, and made a beautiful infield. The players loved it. I did the same thing with home plate, which was all clay. I just mixed the proper ingredients, the proper soils, and made a good home plate area. That's what it takes if you want to satisfy your ball players. And to have happy ball players, your playing surface has to be in Grade A shape.

I was always recognized as one of the better groundskeepers in the Texas League. Above all, you must take pride in your work. It's really rewarding when your players are all happy, and this helps give them the proper attitude toward playing good games. I remember Billy Williams and Ron Perranoski always liked the field conditions in Mission Stadium. Billy Williams was a pretty fast outfielder, so I used to cut the grass short so the ball could get to him quicker. Whereas the fellow in left field wasn't so quick, so I used to let the grass grow high there. This would allow the ball to slow down and he would be able to cut the ball off before it got to the wall. You have to realize in taking care of fields the most important thing is knowing your players, what they can and can't do, then fine-tuning their playing area to their likes, to get the best of their abilities. Ron Santo and Brooks Robinson always loved the infield down there. I used to ask Brooks, "How's the grass; would you like it cut? Or the dirt around the bag, what can I do to make the playing surface better for you?" My players were the most important part of my job, and I would do anything I could to help them out.

In Cocoa, Florida, with the Astros, I had five ball fields that I built by hand. I was really proud of those fields and I put a lot of time into making the Astro complex one of the best. I was always fooling around with that infield. If a team with a lot of speed and good bunters was in town I would make it a little sandy in front of home plate, cut the grass really short, and slant the base paths in toward the field so the ball would have the effect of rolling uphill along the foul lines.

I remember the first piece of Astroturf was tested in Cocoa, Florida. The Astros had Monsanto Chemical Company develop this Astroturf. They brought about a sixty-foot piece down to Cocoa; it weighed a couple of tons. It took a whole bunch of us to take it off the truck, and we laid it down on field number 3. Paul Richards tried hitting some balls onto it; players tried sliding and fielding on it. Then Paul made the final decision, that it was all right to put it in the Astrodome. As a matter of fact, I still have a piece of the original Astroturf.

Before the Astroturf went to Houston, they left the glass clear on the windows in the dome and tried to grow grass in there. But after several tries the grass would turn brown and have to be painted. There is a chemical used to paint grass that doesn't hurt the grass at all; it just turns it green. When I used to get a few brown spots on my fields, I would use vegetable dye. This makes the grass turn really green.

The Astros have now moved from Cocoa to Kissimmee, Florida, where they built them a beautiful stadium. And now the city of Cocoa is trying like hell to get another major league club to come and train here, but it's a lost cause. I remember I put a new sprinkler system in there and had those fields all manicured with 419 Bermuda grass, and the city has let everything run down. They can't even find the sprinkler system now, and it's a good thing they have a lot of rain there or all the grass would be dead. I've told them I would go out there and locate that system any time they want me to. I put that system in there in 1963. Why, it was a beautiful Toro system, and I kept five ball fields in perfect condition the whole time I was there.

Joining the Texas Ranger organization in 1976, I knew the job would be a challenge, as they had been through three head groundskeepers in three years. The first thing I did at Arlington Stadium was change all the dirt in the infield, put 419 Bermuda grass in, and install a new sprinkler system. They don't get a lot of rain in Texas and it's tough keeping the field in shape, but for nine and a half seasons I managed to keep them pretty happy, both management and players. It's not always easy to please everyone, though, I admit. I worked under several different managers, and all of them wanted the field groomed a certain way.

One night in Texas after a game with the New York Yankees it looked like a pretty nice night. Now usually when you have a pretty good club in, you put the tarp down to protect your field so you won't get rained out. Now about four o'clock in the morning I heard some thunder and lightning. So realizing I hadn't put the tarp down, I immediately put my clothes on and drove over to the stadium. I called my ground crew, and they were surprised to hear from me at four o'clock in the morning. They all came down to the ballpark, and we put the tarp down over the field. About an hour later the rain came pouring down. The ground crew and I slept in the dressing room, and needless to say, we saved the ball game for that day.

That's one thing about being on a grounds crew—you always have to be on alert, and you always have to be in contact with the Weather Bureau, because if you have a sellout crowd and the game's rained out that's a lot of money your club will lose. Plus you take a chance of losing your job immediately. A ball club is not going to put up with you not handling your job well.

That was a sellout crowd that night, and with the Yankees we always packed the ballpark. With Billy Martin in here we always managed to draw a pretty good crowd, so needless to say, I was well protected that day. They played the ball game, and the top brass of the organization wanted to know how I got the ballpark in shape, knowing that I hadn't put the tarp down the night before. They hadn't realized that I had gotten up at four o'clock in the morning, rushed in with the ground crew, and put the tarp down. But if that's what you have to do, then that's what you have to do. You have to take pride in your work. With groundskeeping there are long hours, and you have to remember the ball club has a lot of money invested and you have to be able to do your job at all times.

You take a player like Nolan Ryan, who is making more than a couple of million dollars a year. You just can't make any mistakes like leaving the tarp off the field at night. You have to be alert and cautious and take no chances on the field getting soaked overnight. This reminds me of when we had the small tarps. All we could cover was home plate and the pitcher's mound and you might have a couple of tarps to cover the bases, but you still had the whole infield to take care of. In this case we used a product by the name of Turfus, which absorbs about seven to eight times its weight in moisture. It's a powder and I used a couple of tons a year in Arlington. I used to throw that in the infield, and sometimes in the morning if the field looked like it was a little hard I would put a thin layer over the infield and scratch it in and the ball players would just love the beautiful shape of the field. In the minor leagues you couldn't afford putting Turfus on the infield because the cost was prohibitive when you were drawing eight or nine hundred people per game. A minor league team just can't throw that kind of money away by putting Turfus on the field every time it rains. Another thing in the minor leagues, instead of twelve or fifteen groundskeepers, you've only got four or five, so teams are lucky to play as many games as they actually do in the minor leagues, today.

Observations

As far as groundskeepers go, I would have to say that George Toma of the Kansas City Royals is probably the best in the business, today. George landed that job through Hank Peters, when Hank was the general manager in Kansas City. I used to know Hank when I was scouting for the St. Louis Browns. I knew Hank back when he was the general manager in the Iowa State League at Burlington, a Class A organization, which is why today Hank is the general manager for the Cleveland Indians.

It was a real coincidence that when Hank was with the Kansas City Royals he asked me to come in and talk with him about the head groundskeeper job in KC. But the field manager for the Royals at the time had been a manager in the minor leagues in the same ballpark where George Toma had done a great job, so George was highly recommended and that eliminated me.

Now it wasn't too long after that that the Baltimore Orioles were in need of a head groundskeeper. Jim McLaughlin, who was the Orioles' farm director, paid my expenses to fly to Baltimore. Jim and Jack Dunne interviewed me, and as it turned out, Jack offered me less than I was making at San Antonio, so I turned the job down. I really didn't care for Baltimore too much. I was used to living in a smaller city, and Baltimore is a big city, especially compared to where I was living at the time in San Antonio. I really didn't want to move my family and my wife really liked San Antonio, so I turned down the job.

At that time Pat Santarone was the head groundskeeper in Elmira, New York. Earl Weaver was managing in Baltimore, and Earl recomended Pat for the job there. Earl had liked Pat's work in New York when Earl was managing up there. Pat's a really good groundskeeper.

I'd have to say in my opinion, outside of George Toma, Pat is probably the best, and then I'd say there's Joe Mooney with the Boston Red Sox and the Bossards in Chicago and Cleveland. The bottom line on groundskeeping is keeping your players satisfied at all times.

One thing I would like to say to all you managers, including Little League managers and college managers, and coaches alike. Remember when you walk out on that field always check your grass. Check your infield grass to see if it's cut short or long. Check your base paths; see if the ball rolls fair or foul. Check around home plate and the pitcher's mound; try to make the field work toward your team's strengths.

Six
My Favorite Players

Throughout my long association within the game of baseball, I have felt blessed to work in a profession in which all my childhood dreams came true. Having been associated with some of the greatest names in the history of the game and calling them my friends, this, I will tell you, is a dream come true.

I feel proud to have had a job that meant so much to management, coaches, and players, for my performance reflected their performance and we were a group of men with hearts of little boys striving for a common goal.

I have worked with some great talent, and I would have to say my favorite ball player of all time would have to be Brooks Robinson. I remember after every ball game Brooks would come over to my house in San Antonio. We would buy doughnuts and have a doughnut party. He was like a brother, or rather, I loved him like a father loves a son. I'm sure everybody in the world would love to have a son like him. Brooks was an all-American guy. He never complained about his job, and wow, would he make some spectacular plays you wouldn't believe.

"We called John the little round man," Brooks speaks of me fondly. "I was single and nineteen years old when I came up with Baltimore through San Antonio. John was one of my favorite people; he'd come up to me with his sparkling brown eyes and ask, 'Do you want the grass cut or let it grow? How about the ground around the bag at third base?' John was always trying to please the people he was around. Anything anyone needed, John would do his best to have it done. Thanks John."

Buddy Bell, cut from the same mold as Brooks Robinson, is another great guy. Why, every night after the ball game I would go into the clubhouse and talk with him about how the field was. I was always concerned with his feelings about the field condition. Buddy was a great person to be around. He is a great family man with a wonderful family. His dad, Gus Bell, who was a great outfielder in the major leagues, would come and visit. He was always cordial and would talk to you like a long lost friend. Buddy's brother Tim used to play golf with me quite a bit. The Bell family, a class act.

"When I went to Texas the first thing I noticed about John was how much he cared about the field. John really didn't get any consideration from the front office. He was on a very low budget; just about everything he did for the field he did on his own. John was a very hard worker and very knowledgeable about the game. John drove a big Caddy around, so I thought he was getting paid pretty well," Buddy remembers.

"I remember one day we were holding a baseball clinic before our workout and my sons were following me around the different circuits. Now John was kicking all the kids off the field. He kept saying, 'Okay, boys, off the field.' Now I wasn't too far from my son Michael. I saw John bend down to talk to him and Michael just punched John right in the nose. We laughed about that pretty hard in the clubhouse later.

"We always had a good time with John. He was very conscious of his field; he was always making sure it was in excellent playing condition. After all, I did win six Gold Gloves playing on his field. I feel honored to have worked with John and proud to call him my friend."

Bucky Dent was another great guy to be around. One thing I liked about Bucky was that he would always let you know where he stood at all times. I liked to talk to him about the infield; he would let me know if his area at shortstop needed more or less water. During infield practice before games Bucky would get the feel of the infield. I always made sure he was satisfied with his playing surface. In my thirty-five years of baseball he's the only guy who left me with a present at the end of the season.

"I first met John when I was with the Yankees coming into Texas Stadium to play," Bucky recalls. "I used to talk with him. After I was traded to the Rangers from the Yankees we chatted and became good friends.

"Once I started working with John I could tell he was very conscious about his field. I was very particular about my position at shortstop. John would do anything I wanted to make my area perfect for me. That area was my life and my job, so I was very particular, and Johnny did a great job for me. John was a good man. You have to take care of those ground crews; they're your life."

The first time I met Harry Dalton, I went to Thomasville, Georgia, to fix the fields for the Baltimore Orioles' spring training facility. There were different meetings going on and they had a nice recreation room and I would talk to Harry there. I took a liking to Harry the first time I met him. We worked a couple of years together in Baltimore. Harry was a young guy when I first met him; he was the assistant farm director for Baltimore.

We used to meet at the winter baseball meetings and go out for a couple of drinks. I liked Harry; he treated me with respect, and we became good friends. I always kind of kept in contact with him, and I always kept Harry informed of any up-and-coming talent.

"Johnny was an excellent groundsman. Wherever he was

he did a great job. Those groundskeepers are very jealous of their properties and their grasses. John did a great job and was very conscientious and always gave 100 percent. He scouted two years in the Midwest for us. Thanks, John, for a job well done, your friend, Harry Dalton." What a great remembrance!

Eddie Robinson was one of the best general managers I ever worked for. I've been around Eddie so long, he considers me one of his family. I worked with Eddie when he was with the Atlanta Braves; he made me the general manager in Richmond.

When Eddie became the general manager for the Rangers he immediately saw he needed a head groundskeeper, and I was the first one he called.

Eddie is a great human being; he's very considerate of his help. As long as you did a good job for him you never had to worry about your job. Eddie's son Drew worked for me on the ground crew in Texas. A bright young man, I consider him one of my sons.

"I first heard about John in San Antonio. John was the head groundskeeper. He did a great job and was well liked. John was also a good front office man, and when it came to playing golf you might say John was a hustler. When John worked in San Antonio he knocked the general manager on his ass; that story followed him around.

"I didn't waste any time bringing him into Texas. I knew if anybody could fix Texas Stadium, Johnny could. Johnny was a very nice person and was always making his budget. We liked that because we didn't have the money to spend. John was like family to me. He was good to my mom and visited with her often. John is a special person and will always be part of our family," Eddie remembers.

Don Zimmer was one of the best managers I ever worked with. To prove I was right, as soon as he was fired by Eddie Childes, he went right to work for Jim Frye and the Chicago

Cubs. He won the pennant and always put a top team on the field. With the knowledge of baseball that he has, he'll never have to worry about having a job in the game. Don's now a coach with the Boston Red Sox. He's a good family man; his wife used to go to all the ball games. He's a delightful person to be around; I really loved working with Don.

"I first met John in the Florida State League, I was managing Key West, and John was working for the Cocoa Astros. I always got along with the ground crew. As I was a manager, anything I asked them to do they would do. So it was important to keep a good rapport with the ground crew; we worked for the same goals," Don says.

"I remember sitting in the front seat of a bus driving back down to the Keys and our bus driver looked like he was falling asleep at the wheel. We almost hit this blueberry pie truck. I said, 'Pull over,' and asked the players if anyone could drive a truck or bus. Well, Victor Olberry, a pitcher, ended up driving the bus and we later found out that the bus driver had an alcohol problem.

"John was a very good groundskeeper, and with the heat in Texas it's hard to keep the grass in good shape, but I felt John did a fine job, especially under those conditions."

Jim Sundberg is one of the greatest. He has a beautiful family. Jim's the type of guy you want to be around all of the time and a fantastic catcher. I was very disappointed when the Rangers traded him to Kansas City. "Sunny" was one of the most popular players in Ranger history.

"Johnny was always concerned about how the players felt about the field conditions. John worked hard to make sure the field was in the best shape possible. If something wasn't right, all you had to do was let him know and he'd fix it right away. The atmosphere in the clubhouse was very warm towards John; all the guys liked him. He was always pleasant. It was a pleasure working with him. John, thanks," Sunny wrote me recently.

I first met Joe Macko in the Texas League. We hated to see Joe coming into San Antonio. At Mission Stadium, our left field wall was 325 feet and Joe was a real power hitter; he always hit the long ball there. Joe was the equipment manager for the Rangers when I arrived. During the ball games I used to go sit in the clubhouse and talk with Joe. He's one of the finest equipment managers in the American League. Joe really knows the needs and wants of the ball players; he does a great job. That's probably why he's been there from the start.

My greatest concern was when Joe lost his son to cancer, when the boy was playing with the Chicago Cubs. Steve had tremendous ability and would have been in the big leagues a long time.

"I first came to know Johnny when I was twenty-four years old, in 1952. I was a first baseman for the Dallas Eagles in the Texas League. I enjoyed playing at Mission Stadium; I hit a lot of home runs there. The left field fence was to my liking. I remember the sign up on the fence. It was 'I. B. Baumam, Jeweler.' The local jeweler in town gave away wristbands every time someone hit a home run. I hit six home runs in Mission Stadium in one season. I totaled fourteen; I had enough wristbands to last my whole life. I then played for the Tulsa Oilers in 1954 and 1955. I went back to play for the Dallas Eagles in 1956. That's the year our owner passed away and our name was changed to the Dallas Rangers," Joe recalls.

"In 1971 I was the general manager for a minor league club, the Dallas/Forth Worth Spurs of the Texas League. Then in 1972 the Washington Senators moved to Texas and became the Texas Rangers. I am currently the oldest member of the Rangers. John and I have spent a lot of time together and become very close friends.

"John had his own office out beyond center field, but he'd

come sit in my office and we'd talk baseball. There was a special closeness; we could confide in each other. We valued the trust and closeness and built a bond that still lasts today.

"I remember John would be in his golf cart riding around the stadium. Why, one day he was riding along the warning track going to his office and our pitcher, Jon Matlack, was warming up in the bullpen. One of the players threw the ball up real high, and the ball was timed just perfect; you see, that ball came down and went right through the roof of John's golf cart. Startled John so bad, he almost hit the wall in center field. John finally found out that Steve Comer was the culprit. After he threw the ball he lay down in the bullpen.

"One day John was in my golf cart and we were going down a steep hill to the clubhouse outside the stadium to gate 7. We made a left-hand turn towards the players' entrance. Why, John fell out of the cart and rolled three or four times and landed up against the curb.

"John was a good golfer. He hit the ball straight and far; he had a lot of power. John also had a big appetite; he loved to eat. John and I were pretty close. One thing, if John said he would do something or be somewhere at a certain time, you could count on it being so. We had a lot of good times, memories I'll never forget. Thanks, John."

When I was scouting for the St. Louis Browns, I always made it a point to stop over in Burlington, Iowa. Burlington was a Class A team in the Iowa State League, and Hank Peters was the general manager there. Hank used to let all of the St. Louis Brown scouts bring all their outstanding prospects there to work out. Hank would let us use the ballpark for the final workouts, and from there we would decide whom we were going to sign. I remember after a big tryout camp Hank took us out to dinner at the Moose Lodge in Burlington. We then went over to Hank's house, where we met his wife and beautiful daughter. I really appreciated everything Hank did for me. He was a terrific man who treated everyone equally and fairly. Thank you, Hank.

"I first met John with the St. Louis Browns. He lived in Iowa and was an assistant scout in the late 1940s. It was in the fall of 1946 that I started working for the Browns. When the Browns were sold to Baltimore, I didn't make the move until later," Hank recalls.

"I knew John as a scout, general manager, and groundskeeper. John started in the landscaping business in Iowa. John always had a love affair with the game. He's short in stature but big in heart. We go back a long time."

Billy Hunter was very easy to get along with; he seldom made any demands. Billy would just look out on the field. If it was in shape he would leave you alone; if he wanted anything special he would come up and tell you. You always knew where you stood with Billy. And of course when Rick Honeycutt was pitching I always had a special demand from Billy; soften up home plate.

I remember Billy when he played with Baltimore. Why, he was an outstanding shortstop. Billy used to be one of those fancy guys; when he was taking infield practice he would throw the ball sidearm to first real fast. But boy, was he good.

Billy recalls, "I remember we opened up the '78 season with the Yankees. Now my infielders were not the greatest range people, so I suggested that we slope the base paths for bunting so the ball would roll fair. We liked home plate soft; I remember handing in the lineup cards and Billy Martin's shoe went into the sand at home plate over the top of his shoe. I had to have Johnny go out there with his wheelbarrow, tamper, and rake. I told him not to take too much out, just a shovel or two. Dick Butler, the supervisor of umpires, told me, 'Lee McPhail told me to tell you to fix home plate.' I said, 'When Kansas City puts in grass, we'll fix it.'

"As part of our act, we'd come in, cut the ball off after the catcher threw down to second. He almost took off Vern Stephens's head one game. In those days we didn't win a lot of games, but we had fun.

"Bert Campaneris was the best bunter in baseball. He had forty-four sacrifice bunts, while the White Sox as a team only had thirty-six. Eddie Robinson and Brad Corbett were mad because I had Campy bunting and I wasn't letting him swing away. But my philosophy was let's do what's best for the team. I enjoyed my stay at Texas, and Johnny did a great job for us."

Randy Galloway was one of the most outstanding newspaper personalities that I've ever met, and I've met a lot of them. Randy printed it just like it is. He's not a poison pen; he'll give you credit if credit is due and he'll tell you it isn't if it isn't. Dallas is a tough, competitive city for covering sports, and it's not easy with all the professional sport teams in town. The Dallas Cowboys, Mavericks, Rangers, pro golf and tennis, and add in high school and college sports, and you can see Randy is always on the go. I have a lot of respect for him.

"I first met John when I was a beat writer with the Rangers in the early 1970s. There were always a lot of complaints about the field conditions by the Ranger players and other teams' players. Then Eddie Robinson told us that he had someone who could fix this and along came Johnny O. Now, the Ranger ownership didn't have big purse strings. I said I hope he came here with an army, because he has a war on his hands with this field. Johnny shaped the field up to the point where the complaints stopped coming. Now nobody in any profession gripes like ball players over the field conditions. I also liked Johnny's personality; he's one of the best guys you'll ever run into in the business. John has a storehouse of knowledge with all the people and associations he's had in the industry. I'd like to say, John, don't feel bad; look what happened to Tom Landry. If it happened to him it could happen to anybody." A great guy, Randy!

Clint Hurdle had a tremendous personality; all the ball players liked him. He did a great job for us at Cocoa as our batboy. Little did I realize that Clint would pursue his baseball career. I didn't know he would continue, much less become a very popular major leaguer. I have a nice autographed picture of Clint saying I was his first boss. I believe Clint will eventually become the manager of the New York Mets.

"It was around 1967 in Cocoa, Florida. I was very impressed by the entire situation. That was the big leagues to me at the time. John was very important. He was always out on the field; he put a lot of time and effort into the Astros' complex. I've always had a warm feeling towards John and his personality. He was always trying to help make things perfect," Clint remembers.

"Just being around the whole situation was exciting. Add being around John Mayberry, Bob Watson, Stan Pappi, and Steve Hertz and the rest of the ball players. For a young kid that left quite an impact on me. I was there with the Cocoa Astros off and on for three years. The preparation and detail and all the intricacy that goes on, on the inside, were very exciting to me. I'll never forget my days in Cocoa."

The name "Doug Rader" puts a smile on my face. One of the best people to be around and easy to get along with. I first met Doug in Amarillo, Texas. The next time I saw Doug was with the Astros for spring training in Cocoa. Now Doug loved jokes; he played them on everybody. Doug liked to play golf. Why, I remember one day he went out to the Rockledge Country Club and John Bateman was driving with Doug. Hole 15 has this nice little lake in front of the green; it's a par 5. Doug and John were right in front of the lake, and Doug backed the cart right up to the lake. Doug then hit his ball right onto the green, grabbed his putter, and walked over the bridge to the green. John hit this little chip shot onto the green, walked over to the golf cart, hopped in, hit the pedal, and went backwards into the lake. I guess John didn't know Doug had left the cart in reverse. Boy, Doug thought that was really funny. We played a lot of golf together at the Rockledge Country Club.

Later when I was with the Texas Rangers I remember after Darrell Johnson finished the year out as manager, the Ranger management was talking to Doug Rader. Well, I talked with Joe Kline and told him what a great baseball man Doug Rader is and how I thought he would make us a really good manager. Joe Kline interviewed several other potential managers, but when his final decision was made, he came up with Doug Radar. After Doug was appointed manager he thanked me for all the kind words. I just knew Doug was the right man for the job and there wouldn't be a dull moment around here.

I go way back with Mr. Doug. He has a tremendous knowledge of the game. Doug's one guy who never backed down from anyone and always expected 100 percent from everyone at all times. I enjoyed his family; they were always at the games. His wife is a very delightful person, with a very nice son and two beautiful daughters.

"I came up through Amarillo, Texas. It was right after I came to Cocoa, Florida, that I became friends with John Oliveria. I was at spring training with the Houston Astros. John was a good groundskeeper. He had a nice personality, and he was always pleasant to be around.

"I liked to have a good time and joke around. I still think John Bateman may have known that golf cart was in reverse. It was a pleasure being in Texas, and I owe John a bit of gratitude. Johnny O. always tried very hard; he did a fine job with what he had. We all appreciated John. Things got sour when they let John go, but I guess that's the nature of the business. An unjust thing, but what's most important is that John's truly a good friend." Kind words from a great guy.

Marc Holtz is probably one of the best announcers in the American League. Marc knows the business; he's a straight shooter, one of the nicest people I've ever had the pleasure of being around. Marc's lovely wife and beautiful daughter would come to the games. Marc's daughter would go up to the broadcoast booth and listen to her dad broadcast the games. I treasured the times I associated with Marc and his family.

"I used to run into John from time to time. John was one of those behind-the-scenes characters. He knew the game; he was a nuts-and-bolts baseball guy. John knew the subtleties of the game, the height of the foul poles, the pitcher's mound, infield dirt, those little insights to pass along to the listener. John listened to the games; there was a common interest there.

"I remember John would drive around the field in his golf cart. He also had a big Caddy with the license plate 'Johnny O.' He liked to drive. All the players liked him. He was very honest. John knew all the players liked him, and he would take the time to talk to you. We both had a lot of respect for the game.

"John met my wife at a diner. He liked my daughter; at that time she was in her early teens. Whenever I ran into John the first thing he would say was, 'How's the family?' and he would always comment on the broadcast. Most people didn't realize the long hours that John's job entailed. I feel if everybody had John's positive attitude, baseball would be more enjoyable," Marc recalls.

Dave Fendrick and I go back to the Atlanta Braves minor league system. Dave was the general manager for the Savannah Braves Double A team. I was the general manager in Richmond at the time, and Jack McKeon was my manager. I remember one year we were battling for third or fourth place in the International League. Now Dave was fighting for the pennant in Savannah when Jack McKeon decided he needed some help in Richmond. Well, I got the okay from Atlanta and we called up Dale Murphy from Double to Triple A. Jack was happy, but Dave was a little upset. His team is fighting for the pennant and we call up Dale Murphy, who was leading the ball club in everything. Needless to say, Savannah finished the season in second, but I think if they would have kept Dale, they would have won the pennant.

Dave came aboard with the Rangers and we worked together again in the Texas organization. Dave's a great baseball person; he's fun to be around; he really knows the business. I believe he's the promotions director with the Rangers today.

"I remember he did take Dale Murphy from us and we did win our division in Savannah two or three times when I was there. We did get a little upset when they took our players from us, but that's the business. John and I go way back, although he's been in baseball a lot longer than I have," Dave remarks. "He and I were general managers with the Braves organization. It was Eddie Robinson who reunited us in Texas. I was hired as director of group sales."

Rick Honeycutt—the word to describe him is cool, very cool. He was a pretty funny guy, always nice to be around. I would always ask him how the mound was; Rick would always tell me, "Keep the front of home plate pretty soft." Rick was a really easygoing person, a great competitor, truly a first-class individual.

Ferguson Jenkins when he was with the Rangers used to like the grass pretty long between home plate and the pitcher's mound. This made it easier for him to field any little ground balls hit back to the mound; they would slow down in the high grass. Fergie was a great guy to work with; he never complained. He would ask you to do little things now and then, but that was part of the job. He was trying to make a living in baseball. I always enjoyed being around Fergie.

Nolan Ryan is one of the finest gentlemen to put on a baseball uniform. Nolan is not a big head; he's one of the nicest people I've ever been associated with in baseball. And what's truly amazing is that at his age not only is he still pitching, but still throwing smoke. Nolan Ryan, truly a great athlete, one of a kind.

I treasure the people who have crossed my path in this business. I came from a very poor family, but I never gave up. I may not have had a lot of talent as far as playing baseball, but I found it in another area and still reached the major league level. I love the game of baseball and all the people you meet. Why, you know, I've met world-reknowned entertainers, Loretta Lynn, George Gobel, Conway Twitty, and Frank Sinatra, Jr., just to name a few.

I would like to let the young people know they can attain their dreams. You must give 110 percent at all times to reach your goals. Even if you don't have the talent or the tools required for the job, you can still put your knowledge and skills to work for you. Remember, never give up, be honest, treasure your friendships, and do the best at whatever you do. Today is another memory you'll have to treasure the rest of your life.

Best wishes always, John Oliveria.

References

Bierig, Joel. "Comiskey." *The Sporting News* (October 1, 1990): 29.

Blount, Jr., Roy. "Soil Is the Soul of Baseball." *Esquire* (March 28, 1978): 29–30.

———. "Sometimes the Ball Just Takes a Funny Bounce." *Esquire* (August 1977): 17–18.

Bryan, Mike. "Reflections on the Game." *Sports Illustrated* (April 24, 1989): 75–83.

Fimrite, Ron. "A Script Written by God." *Sports Illustrated* (October 17, 1977): 21–23.

Garrity, John. "Nitty Gritty Dirt Man." *Sports Illustrated* (May 17, 1982): 41–49.

Hitzges, Norm. "Dirty Tricks." *Sports Magazine* (August 1982): 58–59.

Hynd, Noel. "Giant-sized Confessions." *Sports Illustrated* (August 29, 1988): 10–12.

McCarthy, Eugene. "Baseball Boingball." *The New Republic* (November 22, 1982): 13–14.

Schuessler, Raymond. "The Tenth Man." *The American Republic* (June 1960): 41–45.

"Swardsmanship." *Newsweek* (June 6, 1966): 86.

Swift, E. M. "There's No Place Like an Old Place." *Sports Illustrated* (July 7, 1980): 53–60.